comets

No More Heroes

David Clayton

Illustrated by
Martin Salisbury

Collins Educational
An Imprint of HarperCollinsPublishers

Published by Collins Educational
77-85 Fulham Palace Road, London W6 8JB

© HarperCollins*Publishers,* 1996

ISBN 0 00 323061 9

Illustration, page layout and cover illustration by Martin Salisbury.
Cover design by Clinton Banbury.

Commissioning Editor: Domenica de Rosa
Editor: Paula Hammond
Production: Susan Cashin

Typeset by Harper Phototypesetters Ltd, Northampton, England
Printed by Caledonian International, Glasgow, Scotland

No More Heroes

Contents

Chapter 1
Man on a Spider

Far out in the North Sea, Nick Dale's dad was working high up on the oil rig that stood, like a giant spider, against the moon.

It had been a quiet night so far. But now danger ran like sparks through the boy's body as he watched his dad work.

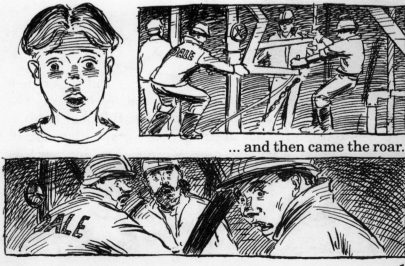

... and then came the roar.

A minute before, the sea had been a sheet of silver steel. Now, a giant shadow ran across it.

A great, dark wave, over a hundred metres high, raced like an express train towards the rig.

Up and up, on and on, it came, its foamy fingers snatching at the air.

Dad, look out!

But the oil men did not move. Suddenly, the wave was upon them. Billions of tons of water blotted out the moon like a great, black ghost.

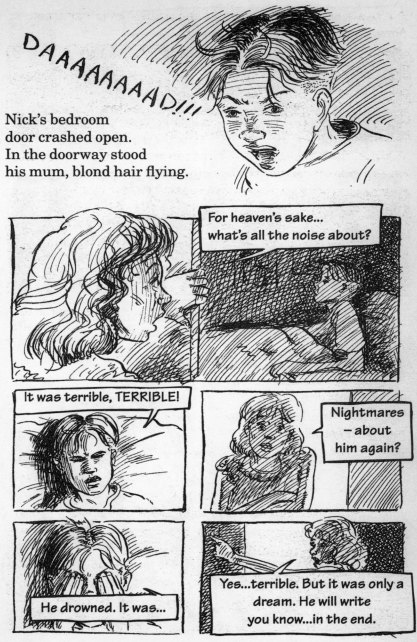

DAAAAAAAAD!!!

Nick's bedroom
door crashed open.
In the doorway stood
his mum, blond hair flying.

For heaven's sake...
what's all the noise about?

It was terrible, TERRIBLE!

Nightmares
– about
him again?

He drowned. It was...

Yes...terrible. But it was only a
dream. He will write
you know...in the end.

I don't want him to just write, I want him...

Back? FORGET IT! We were finished a long time ago.

But..?

Enough! I don't want to talk about it, right?

When she was gone. Nick lay thinking in the dark. Suddenly, a thought popped into his head.

WAS THERE SOMEBODY ELSE? To take his Dad's place? But she wouldn't do that, would she? Take up with somebody else?

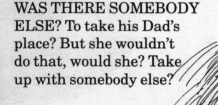

Mum does look nice these days. Looks after herself better...

Maybe I'm too late! I'll have to get in touch with Dad. RIGHT NOW!

Nick jumped out of bed and made for the window. There, past the diamonds of glass scattered over the road, he saw something interesting. Something that gave him hope…Bonzo Brown's big red Granada.

YES! I dug his garden. He owes me one!

BONZO, MY SON, WE ARE GOING FOR A RIDE! SCOTLAND AND DAD HERE WE COME!

At least, that's what Nick thought. But life is never quite that easy, is it?

Chapter 2
The Red Sports Car

On the other side of Scalby, Rockhard Riley was not a happy boy. The night before, his brother Eddy had come in late, and drunk.

Someone's going to get hammered today! Should be Eddy!

NO! He's a psycho! Someone ELSE!

Someone alone. Someone like NICKY DALE!

YEAH!!!

Meanwhile, Nick was making *his* plans.

1. Search the house for Dad's address.
2. See Bonzo Brown – at dinner??? No he'll be drunk – NOW.
3. Sell guitar at the second-hand shop...

Well, look who it is!

Rockhard, Teeth and Big Ben had cut across his path in the last alley before school.

You know what, Dale? You do my head in.

I wouldn't say that, Rock. Nature beat me to it!

Three to one? I'm off!

Going some-where, are we?

ADOLF!

Oh, dear. It appears that you're in for a kicking, son!

But Adolf was too big and clumsy.

Quick as a flash, Nick dipped, twisted, and...

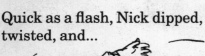

YAAAAA!!

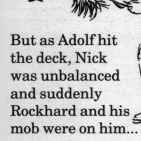

But as Adolf hit the deck, Nick was unbalanced and suddenly Rockhard and his mob were on him...

He felt the first boot go in. THEN...

What was going on?

It's a girl! Get her!

Get real, thickhead! That's DEBBY CHEUNG! She'll snap you in two!

Keep out of this, Cheung! It's him I want!

Get lost, and take the worms with you!

Her eyes were like cold stones. The nutters ghosted away muttering.

By the way, Dale. Saw your mum last night, getting into a red sports car with a hairy greaser. NICE LEGS!

They both laughed.
Nick started to
walk away from
school but he wasn't
laughing inside.

Then, he was alone. Alone with a mind
full of red sports cars, big greasers,
and Dad in Scotland.

Time was running out.

Chapter 3
Unexpected Visitors

It wasn't like Nick to duck out of school. But there was no point in keeping his head down in class today. This greaser story might be true. He had to have his dad's address.

RIGHT NOW!

I'll search Mum's room.

But, ten minutes later, his plan was in tatters. There, parked right outside his house was a car – a red sports car.

His mind went numb. What could he do? Race across the
road, bang on the door and break it up? But his legs
wouldn't move. Suppose...

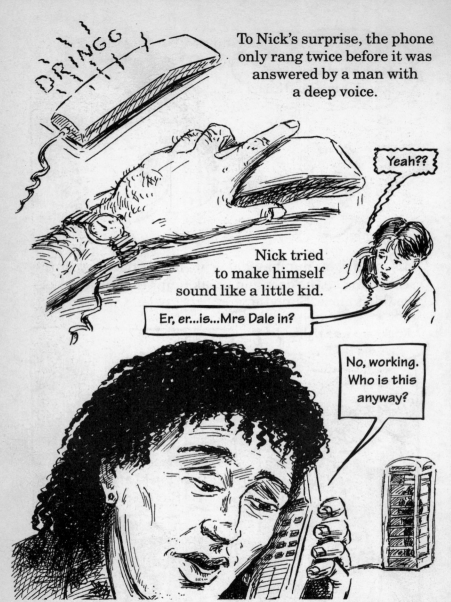

To Nick's surprise, the phone only rang twice before it was answered by a man with a deep voice.

Yeah??

Nick tried to make himself sound like a little kid.

Er, er...is...Mrs Dale in?

No, working. Who is this anyway?

A long silence. This was no use. Frustrated, Nick dropped the phone and bolted across the road to watch the house from a distance.

14

A minute or two later, a tall man with a suntan and dark, curly hair came out of the house. Off he went in the red Porche.

THEN, TEN SECONDS LATER..

What was he doing here on his own? And how come he has a key?

More importantly, where was Dad? Mum said that she didn't have his address anymore, but Nick knew that he sent her money for bills. She had to have his address somewhere. But where?

THINK! THINK! But THINK FASTER!

Chapter 4
Tossing and Turning

One step inside the door Nick stopped. The house was tidy. *Very* tidy. Usually it took you five minutes to find the carpet! Today you could eat off it!

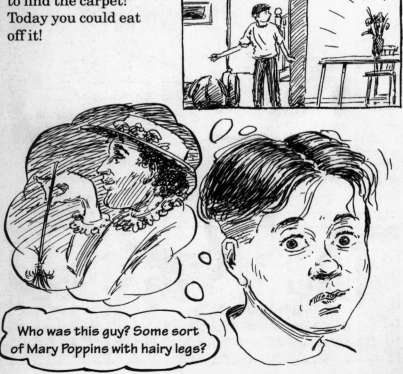

Who was this guy? Some sort of Mary Poppins with hairy legs?

Then he stopped laughing.

The sideboard? No. Kitchen drawer? No. The FORBIDDEN ZONE! Mum's bedroom? HMMM!

Perfume shot up his nose with every drawer he opened.
He found some clothes he'd never seen before.

But NO LETTERS. NO ADDRESS.

Hours later, he had still found nothing. He felt as flat as
a jellyfish – and he still had to tidy up...

Suddenly, the letterbox clattered

Dad's writing!
BINGO!

Chapter 5
The Big Match

Nick soon steamed his dad's letter open. And, right away got a surprise.

Kendal? NOT ABERDEEN! Kendal's only *80* miles from here! Two hours – even in Bonzo's heap!

He would nip up there, clue Dad in about Mr Suntan and bingo! Dad would come back, Mum would give the man with the hair gel the elbow, and they'd all be together again.

BUT when he knocked at Bonzo's door...

He shovelled his computer games, his books, his fishing rod and his guitar into a holdall.

By then it was half past three. Just time to catch the second-hand shop open. BUT...

I'll sell all my stuff and go by taxi.

What's this, Dick Whittington? Running away to London?

Just nipping over to John's.

You're going nowhere right now. WE are going somewhere special tonight. We're watching Scalby Town. For free!

Nick crawled back upstairs, unloaded Santa's sack and had a think.

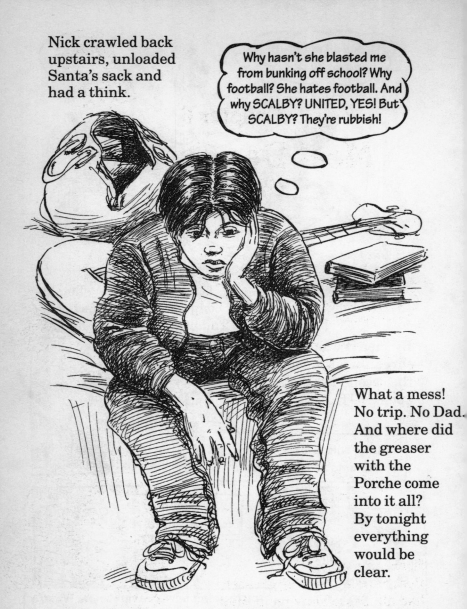

Why hasn't she blasted me from bunking off school? Why football? She hates football. And why SCALBY? UNITED, YES! But SCALBY? They're rubbish!

What a mess! No trip. No Dad. And where did the greaser with the Porche come into it all? By tonight everything would be clear.

And then the trouble would really begin.

Chapter 6
Meet Des Cropper

Bonzo, his mum,
Rockhard and the big greaser
had all messed him up in their
own ways. Only Debby Cheung had been worth
bothering about, but she couldn't get him to Kendal.

By a quarter past six he'd been dressed up in his cleanest jeans and leather jacket.

But when his mother opened the door Nick got a surprise.
It wasn't a red Porche outside but...

...a taxi. And no greaser. Why no boyfriend?
His mum didn't explain.

In no time at all, they were at Scalby's ground. Matches
kicked off at 7.30, but it was still early. What now?

His mum led him past
the terrace turnstile,
past the stand
entrances. Before
he had time to think,
he saw something that
made him go cold.

Oh great! He's a mate of Rockhard
and his loony brother Eddy.

Just then a coachload of Mansfield Town players came in from the car park.

THEN...

Hi, Lisa! And...

Nicky, when he's at home!

Hi, son. I'm Des Cropper

And I'm Eddy Riley.

Nick felt as if he was falling down a deep well. This CROPPER, a friend of the RILEYS, was taking over his mother? No wonder Rockhard had been laughing at him! Suddenly Kendal seemed like the other side of the moon.

Chapter 7
Thinking Time

Although Nick had took the man's hand he did not smile. The man did though. His mum was almost shining. It was terrible. Everybody was happy but him.

Well...better get on with it then.

On with what?

The match. We're both playing... against Mansfield. Don't you know nothing, son?

28

Up and up they went until they were shown into a room with a massive window over the pitch.

The silence was electric. Time passed slowly towards 7.30.

Then came the bombshell.

He'd messed up again. He should have talked to her. Instead he'd given her the silent treatment. Instead of delaying things, he'd pushed her over the edge. Nick's mind was on fire…

She's sold herself. Just because he's a footballer with lots of money! Just because he's big and strong with nice teeth.

Bad thoughts filled his mind…

I hope he gets crippled. She wouldn't want him then, would she? I hope he crashes his car and dies!

NO! Maybe I could prove that he's a crook like Riley? Yes, that would finish him with Mum. She's dead straight.

But it was all just supposes. The whistle blew and the game began.

30

Chapter 8
Face the Music

It was awful.

Des played like a god. Everybody in the ground cheered him – even the Mansfield fans. To cap it all, he went upfield just before half-time. A corner – over it came...

Everybody punched the air, even Nick, until he remembered to be miserable.

Half-time and the crowd were going wild. Cropper was brilliant.

Isn't he wonderful?

Its only a game

You miserable little wimp!

Five seconds later, Nick was off!

All right! To hell with you! Marry Desperate Dan! See if I care!

I'll live with Dad. _He_ won't let me down.

Nick fished about in his pocket for some change for the bus. But...he'd changed his clothes hadn't he? No chance of a trip to Kendal now – and all he had was the leather jacket and a thin shirt to keep him warm on the five mile walk home.

Nick got into the red Porche and in no time they were
heading for Kendal.

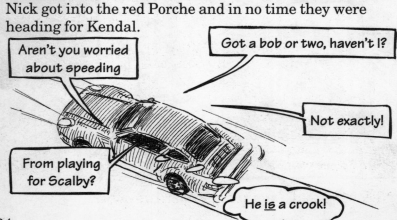

34

Now the footballer was winding him up.

Nick went cold. Another nightmare to have.

Now they were getting close to the Kendal turn off. Soon Des would be out of his life for good. But what if he really was a crook. Where would that leave his mum?

Nick looked at Des' face then shut up. If the man was a crook this wasn't the place to get nosy about it.

Ten minutes off the motorway and they were at his dad's cottage.

The lights were on. He could see shadows inside.

MAYBE...

Chapter 9
Nasty Surprises

Who can that be?

How do I know?

One of the voices inside was a girl's. How could that be? A chain rattled. Orange light glowed out.

What the hell are you doing here?

Who is it?

It's nothing.
I'll sort it out.

But Dad...

Shut up,
for heaven's sake!
She'll hear you!

Dad, it's me,
NICKY!

Who's that?

My nephew, Nicholas.
He's run away from home.

NEPHEW!!!

Well, he
can't stay
here.

You can't do
this to me!

Yes, yes, I'll sort it out.
Go to back to bed.
I'll be back in a minute.

No. You can't do this to
me! You're just like your
mother. Always want
everything your way!

Why do I have to pretend I'm not me!

Because I told this girl I was twenty-seven. You'll understand one day.

Go home to your mother. I can't look after you. Use the phone box at the end of the lane. Get a taxi. There's enough here to cover it.

Nick's dad turned and was gone. The house light went off. The lane was dark and Nick was alone.

That's what I'm worth. A hundred quid!

BUT SUDDENLY.

All right?

Don't ask!

Now I know why Mum didn't want me to see him.

As soon as he flopped into his seat, Nick suddenly felt very tired. The sports car whizzed down the motorway, making the passing lights look like fuzzy rainbows. Nick didn't speak. Couldn't speak.

Des had a quick look at him and left him alone.

An hour later...

Are you all right?

Sort of. A bit let down.

Then blackness ended a dismal day.

Chapter 10
Back to Square One

Yellow light crept through Nick's eyelids. A bird was singing outside. Nick wasn't in a birdy mood. He felt like shooting it.

Then he thought about Des.

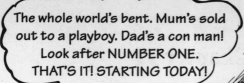

The whole world's bent. Mum's sold out to a playboy. Dad's a con man! Look after NUMBER ONE. THAT'S IT! STARTING TODAY!

Can't let them all get to me.

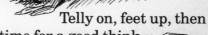

Telly on, feet up, then time for a good think.

Nothing unusual until Nick saw the photofit of the square one.

...security van raid on Dial Road, Scalby. Two men, one strongly built with thick curly hair and a heavy sun tan. A second, square-built...

Eddy Riley!

And the tall one..?

43

Chapter 11
Loot!

By the time the news was over, Nick's mind was buzzing.

SUDDENLY...

Someone was hammering on the front door – loud enough to wake the dead.

It was Eddy Riley, looking like a mad dog.

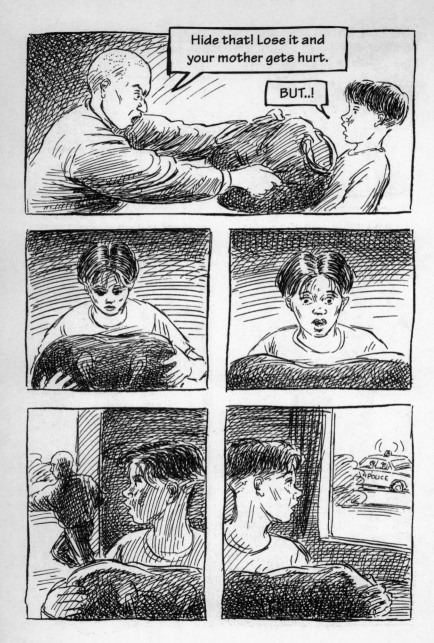

Outside, the 'ch-ch-ch' of the police helicopter and the blare of sirens told Nick why Eddy was in a such hurry. The police were closing in.

BUT NOW HE WAS INVOLVED IN THE CRIME. Should he go to the cops? And get his mother's face slashed?

This bag is bad news. I'll hide it in the wash basket under the stairs.

Is leaving money here part of Des' plan?

Then an even worse thought stopped him in his tracks.

Perhaps Mum knows what's going on!

Chapter 12
Bingo!

When his mum came home, Nick was dying to ask her all sorts of questions. She was smiling and happy.

At the end of the meal, she kissed him and went off to work. Not a word about school. She was too happy to give Nick hassle.

AND NOW, THE BAG!! BUT FIRST – CHECK THE STREET!

NOTHING.

Seconds later he was scrabbling like a maniac at the bag. The zip was locked so he slashed it open with a kitchen knife.

WOW!

He could do anything with this lot. Go round the world, live abroad, visit America. This kind of money would get him and his mum away from Scalby forever! But he couldn't keep it here. He'd have to hide it in one of his secret places. When you don't trust anyone, you have lots of them.

Walker's Mill!

Walker's Mill was five miles up the river through Marple Woods – an old ruin with a mill pond and broken water wheel. Overgrown and secret.

Perfect! But I can't cart it about like this.

A fishing basket caught his eye.

Nobody will bother me if I carry that...stuff the money in the basket and off we go!

He took his rod too, of course. Good to fool people and even better to crack them over the head with!

BUT...

Then...

So that was it then. Nick and his mum were just a safe house for the gang. Nick didn't wait to see any more. He was off and running like a maniac.

Down the zigzag path towards Marple Woods, then into the dark trees beyond...

Chapter 13
Burn Up!

Now the path dived deeper into the forest. Trees towered over head. It was like running into a tunnel. In the dark bushes things were moving, crashing about.

Riley?? And Cropper??

You're dead Dale. You and your mother.

It was Riley. Some how he had followed Nick, and now he was closing in for the kill!

At last he reached the clearing. Ahead he could hear the river's thunder.

BUT, just as he came to the end of the path, a square, wild figure came charging towards him.

GOTCHA!

YAAA!!!!!!!

Riley leapt at Nick, but the footballer didn't know about Nick's karate lessons with Debbie Cheung...

Nick threw the fishing basket into the dark undergrowth and was off — running for his life.

Three hundred metres later he reached the mill. It was a great place to hide. A death trap if you didn't know your way around, but Nick knew it inside out.

They'll never find me here!

He kept a close watch for Riley and Cropper but everything seemed quiet. Outside, the dark clouds grew and grew. Water swished down the broken millrace, and far away, the town lights shone like frosty diamonds beyond the great shadow of the wood.

He lay back and dozed a little.

Suddenly Nick's heart missed a beat.

ALL RIGHT. YOU LITTLE THIEF, LET'S HAVE THE MONEY...OR ELSE..!

Riley again! But Nick knew the game. Get people to shout out and you knew where they were hiding! He'd learned that trick from old war films.

ALL RIGHT THEN, WISE GUY! LET'S SEE IF THIS SHIFTS YOU!

Then something started to tingle his nose. Something started to catch at this throat. Where had he smelt this before?

Then it came to him...
BONFIRE NIGHT!

THE MONEY KID!

A flash of yellow flames and a blast of hot air came rushing up at Nick. Time to die.

If I can just climb up a floor, I can drop into the water...

Can't breathe!

Now the mill was really burning. A massive white and yellow fireball flashed right up one end of the mill and into the roof.

You scumball! Where's the kid?

Up there, but you'll never make it. The boy's a gonner!

Up, up, up! Slowly, so slowly! The skin on his fingers ripped open and the worn rope creaked under the strain.

Can't hold! AAAA!!!!

Then came a black hole in the haze. He swung, grabbed and was in. Into a room.
Ovenheat. No air.

NICK!

Then ONE–TWO–THREE...

They tumbled backwards through space towards the dark waters.

SPLATTT!!!

They were out of the fire, but now there was a new problem. The kid was out cold and the dark whirlpool of the millrace was sucking them in. Des tried a one-handed stroke but his legs were fading. On and on they drifted, closer and closer to the whirlpool at the end of the millrace.

Suddenly...

EDDY!

But still the dark water was pulling, dragging them under.
Four metres, now three. Soon all three would drown.
Two. One.

Hang on!
Help's coming!

I'm going Des...
I'm going!!!

God help me,
Des! AAAAA!!!!

And he was gone.
All the rest was bits and pieces. Like a dream. Lights
were shining. Policemen were coming and going...

We've got you, son!
Charlie take the lad!

Nicky saw none of it. And Eddy? Poor, crazy Eddy? He
was past help – trapped under the dark, fast waters.

It was many weeks before Des or Nick came out of hospital. But, one quiet sunny afternoon...

And they sat and stared at the deep waters again for ages before making their way home.